PROTECTING FARM ANIMALS

PAIGE V. POLINSKY

Consulting Editor, Diane Craig, M.A./Reading Specialist

Sandcastle

An Imprint of Abdo Publishing
abdopublishing.com

abdopublishing.com

Published by Abdo Publishing, a division of ABDO, PO Box 398166, Minneapolis, Minnesota 55439. Copyright © 2017 by Abdo Consulting Group, Inc. International copyrights reserved in all countries. No part of this book may be reproduced in any form without written permission from the publisher. SandCastle™ is a trademark and logo of Abdo Publishing.

Printed in the United States of America, North Mankato, Minnesota

102016
012017

THIS BOOK CONTAINS
RECYCLED MATERIALS

Editor: Rebecca Felix
Content Developer: Nancy Tuminelly
Cover and Interior Design and Production: Mighty Media, Inc.
Photo Credits: Helga Esteb/Shutterstock Images, Shutterstock Images

Publisher's Cataloging-in-Publication Data

Names: Polinsky, Paige V., author.
Title: Protecting farm animals / by Paige V. Polinsky.
Description: Minneapolis, MN : Abdo Publishing, 2017. | Series: Awesome animals in their habitats
Identifiers: LCCN 2016944679 | ISBN 9781680784268 (lib. bdg.) | ISBN 9781680797794 (ebook)
Subjects: LCSH: Animals--Habitations--Juvenile literature. | Habitat (Ecology)--Juvenile literature. | Wildlife conservation--Juvenile literature.
Classification: DDC 577--dc23
LC record available at http://lccn.loc.gov/2016944679

SandCastle™ Level: Transitional

SandCastle™ books are created by a team of professional educators, reading specialists, and content developers around five essential components—phonemic awareness, phonics, vocabulary, text comprehension, and fluency—to assist young readers as they develop reading skills and strategies and increase their general knowledge. All books are written, reviewed, and leveled for guided reading, early reading intervention, and Accelerated Reader™ programs for use in shared, guided, and independent reading and writing activities to support a balanced approach to literacy instruction. The SandCastle™ series has four levels that correspond to early literacy development. The levels are provided to help teachers and parents select appropriate books for young readers.

EMERGING · BEGINNING · TRANSITIONAL · FLUENT

CONTENTS

ABOUT FARMS

Farms are places where people raise animals.

There are many
kinds of farms.

Pigs live on **pork** farms. They are raised for their meat.

Some cows are raised for their meat too. They live on **beef** cattle farms.

Temple Grandin is an animal **behaviorist**.

She studies cows. She helps
farmers make their cows more
comfortable.

Some cows live on dairy farms.

We drink their milk. It is also used
to make butter and cheese.

Poultry farms raise turkeys and chickens. We eat their meat.

Egg farms raise chickens too.
The farmers sell their eggs.

Hobby farms are small.

Hobby farmers raise animals such as horses for fun.

Factory farms are very large. There, animals are packed inside buildings.

They don't have room to move
around. Many get sick.

Farms are very important. They give us our food.

But all farm animals should be treated well.

Responsible farmers take good care of their animals. And you can help them!

Ask where your food comes from.
Buy from small family farms when
you can.

THINK ABOUT IT

Have you ever visited a farm?
What animals did you see there?

GLOSSARY

beef – the meat from a bull, ox, steer, or cow.

behaviorist – a person who studies animal behavior.

comfortable – providing physical comfort.

pork – meat that comes from a pig.

poultry – birds, such as chickens or turkeys, raised for eggs or meat.

responsible – able to be trusted to do an important duty.